THE SCIENCE MUSEUM
BOOK OF AMAZING FACTS

TIME

Dr Mike Goldsmith has been interested in science, and especially the study and measurement of time, for many years. He studied the philosophy of time and space at Keele University, where he also obtained his Ph. D. in astrophysics. He has investigated stars, sound and speech, and now works at the UK's National Physical Laboratory, which is the source of the national time standard.

Many of the amazing facts in this book were inspired by exhibits in the SCIENCE MUSEUM in London. It is home to many of the greatest treasures in the history of science, invention and discovery, and there are also hands-on galleries where you can try things out for yourself. If you live in the North of England visit the Science Museum's outposts, the National Railway Museum in York and the National Museum of Photography, Film & Television in Bradford.

Published by Hodder Children's Books 1999

10 9 8 7 6 5 4 3 2 1

A Catalogue record for this book is available from the British Library

ISBN 0 340 73625 9

Designed by Fiona Webb
Cover illustration by Ainslie MacLeod

Hodder Children's Books
A division of Hodder Headline plc
338 Euston Road
London NW1 3BH

Printed and bound in Great Britain by
The Guernsey Press Company Limited,Guernsey,C.I.

Sci√m

THE SCIENCE MUSEUM BOOK OF AMAZING FACTS

TIME

SCHOOL
THE WEEK WAS INVENTED SO THAT THEY CAN GET RID OF US FROM MONDAY TO FRIDAY...

MIKE GOLDSMITH

ILLUSTRATED BY CHRISTINE ROCHE

Hodder Children's Books

a division of Hodder Headline plc

With thanks to Gerd Nissen, Ian Fowler and John Davis.

THE DATE?
HUMMM.... ACCORDING TO THE NILE THIS MORNING...
AND the STARS...
AND THE FACT THAT it's BEEN FOUR FULL MOONS SINCE THE DEATH OF RAMESES...
EGYPT

Contents

I MAKE it 6 steps — we've Got plenty of time.
AND I MAKE it 12 AND WE'RE LATE!

CHAPTER 1

Mysteries of time

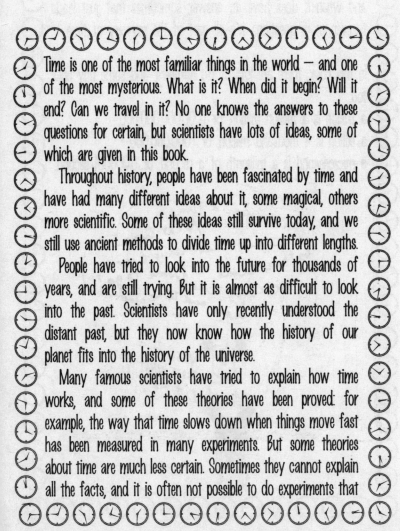

Time is one of the most familiar things in the world – and one of the most mysterious. What is it? When did it begin? Will it end? Can we travel in it? No one knows the answers to these questions for certain, but scientists have lots of ideas, some of which are given in this book.

Throughout history, people have been fascinated by time and have had many different ideas about it, some magical, others more scientific. Some of these ideas still survive today, and we still use ancient methods to divide time up into different lengths.

People have tried to look into the future for thousands of years, and are still trying. But it is almost as difficult to look into the past. Scientists have only recently understood the distant past, but they now know how the history of our planet fits into the history of the universe.

Many famous scientists have tried to explain how time works, and some of these theories have been proved: for example, the way that time slows down when things move fast has been measured in many experiments. But some theories about time are much less certain. Sometimes they cannot explain all the facts, and it is often not possible to do experiments that can prove or disprove them, so they may be improved or completely replaced one day.

So modern science does not have all the answers to time – and when it does have an answer, sometimes that just leads to even more questions: it's all part of the mystery of time.

In this book, there are lots of big numbers, and some tiny ones too:
a trillion is a million million, or 1,000,000,000,000;
a billion is a thousand million, or 1,000,000,000;
a microsecond is a millionth of a second, or 0.000001 second.

once upon a time...
Next time-
I don't have any time!
is there time?
time to go!
Some other time...
time and time again...
YES... BUT WHAT IS TIME?

CYCLING THROUGH TIME

Everything that has happened will happen again. This is what the ancient Maya and many other early civilisations thought: that time went round in a circle and everything repeated itself. They probably got this idea from seeing that in nature many things are repeated over time – the tides, the seasons, animals, and plants all go through cycles of change. A few scientists think that the whole universe really might be created and destroyed over and over again, over periods of hundreds of billions of years.

LIVER FOR TOMORROW

I'LL TELL YOU WHAT YOUR FUTURE HOLDS IF YOU DON'T EAT THAT LIVER–!

Before you eat liver, have a good look at it – you might see your future looking back at you. The Babylonians used the livers of sheep and goats in their attempts to foretell the future. They were fascinated by horoscopes and fortune-telling and they also tried to use the stars, smoke and dreams to predict what would happen to them (*see* **Tricky predicting**, *page 18, for more about forecasting the future*).

BIRTHDAYS OF DESTINY

If you have a bad day, you could always blame your birthday. The Maya, who originated in Central America over two thousand years ago, thought that the whole of a person's life was determined by the day on which they were born – so they didn't have much choice about what happened to them. It seems that people were even named after the day they were born, and could only marry people with the right birthday.

DIFFICULT DAYS

How many really bad days do you have each year? The Maya knew exactly how many they had: five. Their calendar had eighteen months of twenty days each, which makes 360 days. But the year has about 365 days, and the five left-over days were believed to be especially unlucky and known as 'days left over and profitless'. The Maya had all sorts of other, not-quite-as-bad days too, as well as some good ones: some were 'bad for walking in the forest' while others were 'good for bees'.

WHAT DO YOU MEAN, WHEN?

Could you do without time? Some people do. The Hopi, a tribe that lives in Arizona, do not have any words for 'past', 'future', 'tomorrow' or 'yesterday.' Other tribes have different views of time: the Azande of the Sudan think of the future being part of the present, and the Nuer, also from the Sudan, have no word for 'time', nor any way to describe any lengths of time like hours, minutes or seconds.

THE OLDEST KINGS

In Asia, about 6000 years ago, kings lived a lot longer than they do now – about 30,000 years each. At least, they did if you believe the records left about them. There is a document called the 'Sumerian King List', which lists eight kings who reigned one after the other – for a total of 241,200 years! After this, there was a great flood. The flood was real, but the ages weren't: although many early civilisations were interested in history, the idea of accurate dates is quite a modern one.

THE AGE OF THE WORLD

The world started at 6 p.m. on 24 October 3963 BC – or at least, that's what an astronomer in the seventeenth century said, and lots of people believed him. The trouble was that until the nineteenth century there was no way to work out how old the Earth was. And because people did not understand the way the Sun worked, they thought that it could not have been shining for more than a few million years, so the Earth could not be older than this. Measurements of Moon rocks and meteorites, which we know are about as old as the Earth, have now fixed the age at about 4.6 billion years.

ZOO TIME

Japanese clocks used animals as well as numbers to tell the time. Until about 1873, the only numbers used in clocks were 4,5,6,7,8 and 9 – not enough for all the hours, so each number had to be used four times a day. To avoid confusion, animals were associated with hours as well as numbers: so noon was represented by a horse, and midnight by a rat.

WHAT SIGN ARE YOU?

DID YOU KNOW YOU'RE REALLY A GEMINI AND NOT A CANCERIAN?
AH! THAT EXPLAINS EVERYTHING!
HOROSCOPE

You're not the sign you think you are! If you were born on, say 12 July, you may think you are a Cancerian. But really you are Gemini! According to astrologers, whatever group of stars is behind the Sun when a person is born is their sign of the zodiac. But because of slow changes in the position of the Earth, the star-groups that are behind the Sun at a particular time of year are not the same as they were when astrology was invented, so the dates given in horoscopes for each sign are wrong. There is good scientific evidence that astrology does not work, and psychologists have found that people agree with almost anything good that is said about them. Horoscopes are full of good news, so it is not surprising that people like to believe in them.

MONSTERS IN THE ROCKS

There are monsters under your feet! For centuries, people have found the remains of weird creatures in rocks. As well as dinosaurs, there is a creature with five eyes and a single claw, and another called *Hallucigenia* (which means 'bizarre and dream-like'), that had six small tentacles, fourteen legs, and seven big tentacles – each containing a mouth! Luckily these creatures are only a few centimetres long – at least, the ones that have been found so far ... Until quite recently, the ages of these creatures was a mystery, but now we know that they are hundreds of millions of years old.

THE MYSTERY OF THE MISSING LINK

I TELL YOU—THERE ARE NO MISSING LINKS—

Early this century, scientists were searching for a 'missing link', an ancient creature half-man and half-ape which scientists thought was the animal from which the earliest humans evolved. In 1912 the remains of one of these creatures were found in Sussex. It had the skull of a human and the jaw of an ape, and was called 'Piltdown Man' after the place it was found.

At first, people thought that it was more than 100,000 years old, but in 1949 scientists discovered that the skull was not as old as it seemed, and by 1953 it was clear that the Piltdown Man was a fake – the jaw really did belong to an ape and the skull to a man. Scientists could date the bones by measuring the amount of fluorine in them, because bones slowly draw in this substance from the soil (*see* **How old is that glow?** *page 103 for other ways to date things*). The identity of the person who made the fake creature is still a mystery.

INSECTS OF DEATH

You can tell how long a corpse has been dead by what is eating it. If it has only recently been killed, police scientists can estimate the time of death from its temperature. After a few hours, the body starts to stiffen, and then a day or so later it becomes soft again. Flies will soon lay eggs on it, and the eggs hatch into maggots which grow in size over a few days, with some types growing faster than others. So scientists can date the body from the size and type of maggot eating it. They can date bodies that have been dead for years by measuring the amounts of different substances in them. In 1983, a woman's head was found in a peat bog, and a man confessed to murdering his wife twenty years before. But in fact the head was about 1770 years old!

TIME'S ARROW

The most obvious thing about time is the most difficult to explain. Use a watch or clock to time a minute: before you started, that minute was part of the future, but as soon as you finish, it has become part of the past. Now try remembering tomorrow, or having something different for lunch yesterday – tricky, isn't it? The universe, our minds, and the laws of nature all move in one direction, from past to future. So time behaves like an arrow, and the amazing fact is that scientists have so far found it impossible to explain why.

INTO THE FOURTH DIMENSION

You are travelling through the fourth dimension: time. Albert Einstein, one of the greatest scientists of all, realised that time is very similar to space. So sometimes time is called the fourth dimension – the other three are the space dimensions: up/down, forward/backward, and right/left. Normally we can only choose where we go in space, and spend our lives moving steadily in one direction through time. But there *are* ways to change our movement through time (*see* **Time for everyone**, *page 19*, **Warp factors**, *page 110 and* **Stopping time**, *page 111*).

TRICKY PREDICTING

Weather forecasts are impossible! Sometimes the future is easy to foretell (like what time it will be if an elephant sits on your fence*), but other things – like the weather – are impossible to predict, except very roughly, and for a short time in the future. The problem is that the weather is affected by all sorts of tiny things, and no one knows which of them will turn out

(time to get a new fence)*

to be important. This means that, if the same weather information is fed into slightly different computers, they will come up with completely different forecasts. This is called the 'butterfly effect', from the idea that a butterfly flapping its wings in one part of the world could lead to a storm somewhere else.

TIME FOR EVERYONE

Everyone has their own time. Albert Einstein discovered that no two clocks – or people – keep exactly the same time. It depends on how fast they are moving: the hands of a clock moving past you will turn more slowly than those of a clock standing next to you, and the faster the clock moves past, the slower its hands turn. This is not something that just affects clocks: time really does slow down when things move. On the Earth, things move quite slowly, so these effects are tiny, but it is possible to measure them in fast planes. In the future, space travellers might make high-speed journeys which only take them a few years, but return to Earth to find that centuries have passed there (*see* **Backwards in time**, *page 21, for more about how speed affects time*).

TIME AND FATE

Do you feel like being impossible? Try this: go back in time, find one of your grannies when she was a baby, and murder her. This sounds easy (except for the first bit!), but if she was murdered as a baby,

she could not have had any grandchildren – so where did you come from? You could never have been born. But if you were never born, you couldn't have gone back in time and killed your granny, so she would have survived and you *would* have been born, gone back, killed her, not been born ... This kind of impossible situation has put some scientists off the idea of time-travelling altogether, but others say that not only is time-travel possible, they know how to do it (*see* **Time machines**, *page 112*).

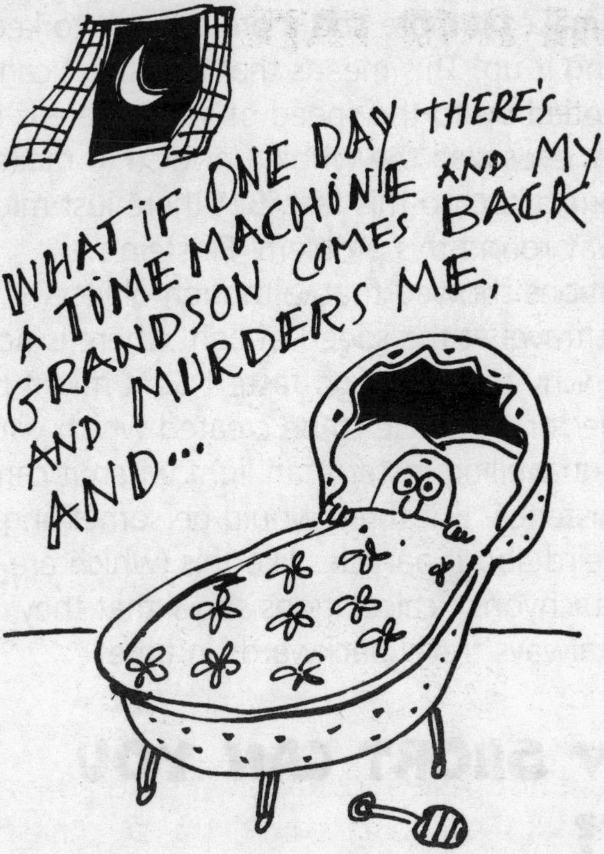

WHAT IF ONE DAY THERE'S A TIME MACHINE AND MY GRANDSON COMES BACK AND MURDERS ME, AND...

BACKWARDS IN TIME

Human beings can't travel backwards in time (not yet, anyway) – but some things might do it all the time. Albert Einstein showed that if you try to make an object go extremely fast, something strange happens to it: it starts to get heavier. The faster it goes, the heavier it gets, which makes it more and more difficult to keep speeding it up. This means that no object can be speeded up to the speed of light: there is not enough energy in the whole universe to make even one atom go this fast. But there just might be a way round this problem: Einstein's calculations showed that, although objects cannot travel *at* the speed of light, there is no reason why they can't go faster! So it might be possible for a particle to be created which was already travelling faster than light when it came into existence. But there would be something very weird about particles like this (which are called tachyons): calculations show that they would always travel backwards in time!

HOW SHORT CAN YOU GET?

There is a time so short that nothing can happen in it. The quickest thing that can be measured is a pulse of laser light that takes 0.000,000,000,000,001 second, but the quickest known change happens in about 0.000,000,000,000,000,000,000,001 second (one millionth of a billionth of a billionth of a second). This is the time taken for a particular type of particle to be destroyed. Scientists think that the shortest possible time is one millionth of a trillionth of a trillionth of a trillionth of a second: however quickly something happens, it has to take at least this long.

LUMPY TIME?

Lots of things come in lumps: houses are made of bricks, water is made of molecules, and time might be made of chronons. If it is, it would mean that everything happens in tiny jumps – jumps so small that no one notices them. This is a bit like the way cinema films work: things happening on the screen look smooth, but actually they move in jumps a fraction of a second long. If time is really made of lumps like this, they must be very small indeed – a millionth of a billionth of a billionth of a second long, or even smaller!

Quiz

1 Moving clocks go
a) Faster than...
b) Slower than...
c) At the same speed... as stationary ones.

2 The fourth dimension is
a) Time
b) Space
c) Up/down

3 The quickest thing that has been measured is
a) A pulse of laser light
b) A particle disintegrating
c) A chronon

4 A chronon (if it exists) is
a) A particle that travels backwards in time
b) A particle of time
c) Very small

5 A tachyon (if it exists) is
a) A particle that sticks things together
b) A particle that travels backwards in time
c) A type of molecule

6 To foretell the future the Babylonians used
a) Liver
b) The stars
c) Smoke

7 In Japan, noon used to be represented by
a) A horse
b) A banana
c) A dragon

8 *Hallucigenia* was
a) A drug
b) A seven-mouthed monster
c) A dinosaur

9 How many really bad days did the Maya have each year?
a) 360
b) 5
c) 1

10 The Earth formed
a) About 15 billion years ago
b) About 4.6 billion years ago
c) In 3963 BC

CHAPTER 2

Telling the Time

'What is time?' is one of the most difficult questions to answer, but 'What is the time?' is one of the easiest – at least, it is now. It has taken centuries of work to come up with today's accurate, cheap and reliable clocks and watches.

The first clocks were simple – sticks and stones that cast shadows in the Sun. As the Earth turned, and the Sun moved across the sky, the shadows changed their shapes and positions, and this provided a rough measure of time. It was a simple idea that worked well – until the Sun went in, or set.

Mechanical clocks were invented in about the thirteenth century. To begin with they were very inaccurate: often by more than a quarter of an hour a day! Then the pendulum was invented and they became much better. The first watches were developed in the late fifteenth century.

Mechanical clocks were fine for everyday needs, but for really accurate purposes, something even better was needed. This century, the quartz clock was invented, and then the atomic clock. From clocks that lost or gained many minutes a day a few centuries ago, we now have clocks that would not lose or gain a second in millions of years.

HOW LONG IS IT TO DINNER?

The Ancient Greeks did not measure time with mechanical clocks or watches – instead they used their feet! In a play called *The Frogs*, written in about 405 BC, a character says, 'When the shadow is ten steps long, come to dinner.' The shadow would have been made by a column, and its length marked off by human foot-lengths. During the morning, as the Sun rose higher in the sky, the shadow shortened, and during the afternoon it lengthened again. Shadow-clocks like these were the first type of clock, and have probably been used for thousands of years.

TWO-TIMING

All sundials are wrong! If you check your watch against one (which you might find in a park or garden, or on a church), you will find that they nearly always disagree. The trouble is that the hours that clocks and watches use are all the same length, but the sundial's hours depend on how the Sun moves in the sky. This is different each day, so the sundial's hours change in length every day too.

STEALING TIME

The ancient Romans were very good at making conquests, but not very good at making sundials. Sundials were as important in ancient cities as public clocks are today, so when the Romans conquered Sicily, they were pleased to capture a sundial to take home with them. Unfortunately they did not realise that, like other sundials, the Sicilian one was designed to work in one place – Sicily. So when it was moved north to Rome it could not tell the time correctly any more, which served the Romans right for stealing it in the first place! The problem with moving sundials around is to do with the position of the Sun in the sky. At a particular time of day (like 4 p.m.) the Sun in Rome is in a different part of the sky than it is in Sicily. This means that shadows in Rome and Sicily at the same time of day are different lengths and point in slightly different directions. So if you made a sundial in Sicily, wrote '4 p.m.' at the place its shadow reached at 4 p.m., and then moved your sundial to Rome, its shadow would *not* point to your '4 p.m.' mark at 4 p.m..

THE 2000-YEAR-OLD TEASMADE

Perhaps you have a clock in your home that makes tea in the morning. It's a nice modern idea, but the first one was built over 2000 years ago – though it delivered milk and wine, rather than tea! It was invented by a famous Greek scientist called Hero, and was a clockwork model of a temple, in which doors opened, drinks were poured, music played and figures danced. Hero also experimented with steam-engines, and his Teasmade, like today's, was steam-driven.

THE SMELL OF TIME

Hundreds of years ago, you could smell what time it was. China and Japan both used fire clocks. These were either candles or containers filled with incense which burnt away slowly, so people could tell the time from the length of the candle or the amount of incense left. Sometimes differently scented incense was inserted at regular intervals, so the smell changed at different times of day. In England more than a thousand years ago, King Alfred used candles to tell the time: it took each of his candles about four hours to burn down completely.

OFF COURSE FOR INDIA

The West Indies got their name because Columbus didn't have a proper clock. He wanted to go round the world to get to the west coast of India, but without a clock he couldn't know how far he was from home. If you went on an ocean voyage like Columbus, it would be fairly easy to find out where you were. At a particular time of day, say 1 p.m., the Sun is seen in a different part of the sky depending on where you are. If you knew that it was 1 p.m. in London you could look at a book to tell you the position of the Sun in the London sky. By comparing this with the position of the Sun in the sky where you were, you could work out how far east or west you were from London. Nowadays it's very simple to find out the time in London, just by looking at your watch. But all Columbus had to tell the time on his six-month voyage was a half-hour sand-glass, like a big egg-timer, which meant he didn't know the time at home and so had no idea where he was. In fact he ended up just east of America, thousands of kilometres from where he thought he was. It took another two and a half centuries to develop clocks good enough to be used for navigation.

THE CLOCK-MONK

The first mechanical clocks were looked after by monks – before that, some clocks *were* monks. The reason monks wanted to know the time is because they had to pray at particular times of the day or night. So, a monk would read the Bible for a set time (measured by a sundial), so that he knew how long it took him to read a certain number of pages. Then, when he read the Bible again, he could tell how long had passed by the number of pages he had read, so he knew when it was time to ring the bell to tell the other monks to pray.

PSST... HOW MANY VERSES BEFORE IT'S LUNCH TIME?

THE LIQUID CLOCK

Most mechanical clocks are made of metals, and one of the very first was too – but one of the metals was liquid! Mercury, the only metal that is liquid at room temperature, was used to make this clock work. Like other early mechanical clocks, a weight pulled a drum round and the drum was attached to a dial to tell the time. The problem was to keep the drum from turning too quickly, and the mercury did this, by weighing down the bottom of the drum. Mercury was used rather than water because mercury is a much heavier liquid.

BAD BEER AND BIG BEN

Six hundred years ago a clock was built in Westminster that people hated – but not because it was noisy or ugly, or wrong. They hated it because it made their beer sour. Or so they said. This clock was destroyed, but a similar one built at about this time for Wells Cathedral is now in the Science Museum in London, and is still working today. Centuries later, after the unpopular Westminster clock had gone, Big Ben was built near the same place. But during the First World War, people didn't like Big Ben either

– this time they thought that zeppelins used its chimes to home in on to bomb London, and they insisted that the clock was silenced.

WHY CLOCKWISE?

Why do the hands of a clock go clockwise? Because a clock is a working model of the solar system.

Some old clocks have a model of the Earth in the middle, a model of the Sun on the hour hand, and stars around the edges of its face. This is how the scientists believed the solar system worked until the sixteenth century, with the Earth at the middle, the Sun going round it, and the stars at the edges.

If you were high above the North Pole of the Earth, you would see the Sun apparently doing just what the hands of a clock do – moving around the Earth 'clockwise'. We now know that the Earth and the other planets go round the Sun, and that the stars are nowhere near the edge of the solar system (even the nearest ones are millions of times further from the Earth than the Sun is).

THE LONG HOURS

Until the fourteenth century, hours were all sorts of lengths: during winter, they were longer at night than during the day. This was because, thousands of years before, the ancient Egyptians decided to have the same number of hours each night and each day. But the lengths of night and day change through the year (*see* **The long night**, *page 83*), so the hours had to stretch and shrink too.

People only started to use hours of a fixed length (called 'equal hours') when mechanical clocks were invented, and for a while both types were used. So, when using these equal hours, people would say 'of the clock', which is why we say 'o'clock' today.

Equal hours were not used in Japan until 1873, so before then Japanese clocks had to have movable hour-markers (*see* **Zoo time**, *page 13, for more about Japanese clocks*).

THE SCIENTIST, THE CLOCK, AND THE BUTCHER

A key moment in clockmaking history happened in the middle of the eighteenth century, in a butcher's shop in Italy. The first accurate mechanical clock was the pendulum clock, and this was invented by Christiaan Huygens, a Dutch scientist, in 1657. Or was it? In 1673 the biographer of Galileo Galilei, the great Italian scientist, claimed that Galileo had invented a pendulum clock before Huygens. No one believed him – but then, eighty years later, an

Italian professor actually found Galileo's plans for a pendulum clock, being used to wrap meat in a butcher's shop! Galileo's son even started to make a clock based on the plans, but no one knows what happened to it.

CLOCKS ON THE MOON

If you took a grandfather clock to the Moon, its hands would turn at less than half the speed they would at home. The speed depends on the clock's pendulum, and the important thing about a pendulum is that it takes the same time to swing from side to side, no matter how much weight is attached to it or how wide the swings are. The only things that change the time of the swing are the length of the pendulum, and the strength of gravity (the force that stops you and everything else from floating away into space).

On the Moon, gravity is about one-sixth as strong as on Earth, so the pendulum slows down. The weak gravity is the reason astronauts seem to move in slow-motion on the Moon – they fall more slowly, and the natural swing of their arms and legs is slower too.

SAILING THE SEAS OF TIME

During the sixteenth century, clocks did much more than tell the time. One clock built in Prague in 1580 was a ship that would sail up and down a table, firing its guns and playing an organ. On board, little people bowed to a model of the clock's owner, Emperor Rudolph II. It had a tiny clockface at the bottom of a mast – which must have been tricky to read when the ship was on the move.

THE DISOBEDIENT CLOCK

Louis XIV, king of France, was so annoyed by his clock that he put its maker in prison. The clock had models of the other kings of Europe that bowed to a model of Louis every hour. The model of the English king, William III, bowed especially low, because the two kings were enemies at the time. Louis was very pleased with the clock until, when it was on show to the public, his own model broke, and fell at the feet of the model of William. Louis sent the clockmaker to prison in the Bastille for a night to punish him for the embarrassment.

THE AMAZING METAL MOUSE

Why do metal mice run round rooms? It's because they're telling the time! A clock was designed in 1650 in which a clock-mechanism moved a magnet around the walls of a room, pulling a metal mouse around. The position of the mouse indicated the time. We don't know whether or not this clock was actually built, but the inventor, Grollier de Servière, did make clocks in which model turtles swam round pools of water with hours marked around them, and lizards climbed columns to tell the time.

ALARMING IDEAS

In the eighteenth century, some alarm clocks didn't ring a bell – they fired a cannon. At the correct time, the Sun's rays would be concentrated by a lens on to some gunpowder, which exploded to fire the cannon. Another type of alarm clock made a spark which lit a pop-up candle. Even sand-glasses were sometimes fitted with alarms: there is one in the Science Museum in London, which tips over at a set time, releasing a clapper to strike a bell.

TICKING FOREVER?

All machines, including clocks, need power to make them work. In 1760 an English inventor called Cox invented a clock that did not need winding. But it still needed power, so it got it from the air – the clock was kept wound up by natural changes in air pressure. There was another clock which really seemed to work without power, from the air or anywhere else. Finally its secret was discovered – the power came from the door of the room it was kept in, so it could only keep working if people kept going in and looking at it!

BIRDS OF TIME

In Russia there is a tree surrounded by birds, animals and mushrooms which tell the time. The mushrooms show the hours and minutes on their caps, and the seconds are shown by a spinning circle of grasshoppers. Each day a peacock opens its tail and bows, and an owl blinks and turns its head. This clock was built over 200 years ago and taken to Russia from England in pieces. It is said that the Russian engineer who was given the job of putting the pieces together again just looked at them all for three weeks. Finally, he discovered that the key to putting the whole clock together was that one of the peacock's tail-feathers was slightly different to the rest.

DANGEROUS TIMES

Why do you wear a wrist-watch instead of a pocket watch as people did a century ago? Because it's safer! The first wrist-watch was made, as a novelty, in 1790, and in 1880 a Swiss company started making more, but they were not very popular. But during the First World War, soldiers in trenches found that it was much less dangerous to glance at watches on their wrists than to stand up in view of the enemy and take them out of their pockets. After the war, lots of people started to wear wrist-watches.

THE DEADLY CLOCK

There was once a type of clock which was quite likely to blow you up – if it didn't dissolve you first. In this clock, pieces of metal were dropped into a container of acid. The metal dissolved and hydrogen gas was given off, which provided the power to operate the clock. Unfortunately, the acid dissolved flesh as well as metal, and hydrogen gas is highly explosive. Luckily very few of these clocks were made.

THE PRICE OF TIME

The most expensive clock was sold for $1,585,475 (about £905,882). It was a mechanical clock made by Cartier, a famous clockmaking and jewellers company, and it was made in 1927 and designed in an Egyptian style. It was sold at an auction in New York in 1991.

TICK TICK OR TICK TOCK?

A clock doctor listens to a clock's tick for the same reason a human doctor listens to your heart. If you have listened to a grandfather clock, or any clock with a pendulum, you have heard it go *tick-tock*. Each time the pendulum swings, it moves the hands round a small amount using cog wheels. The *tick* is the sound of the cogs jumping. When the pendulum swings back they jump again, and make a *tock*. If the *tick* sounds very different to the *tock*, it probably means the clock is not running evenly. This is often caused by the clock not being on a level surface.

STRONG on The TICK-
OFF COLOUR ON The
TOCK...

STICK IT IN THE OVEN, URI

One way to fix a stopped mechanical clock is to put it in the oven. Old clocks sometimes stop when their oil gets sticky with dust and jams up the gear-wheels, and heating the clock in the oven (gently!) makes the oil runny again. In the same way, sometimes holding a stopped mechanical watch in your hand warms it up and starts it going again – which might be one of the secrets of Uri Geller, the conjuror who claims to be able to bend spoons and mend watches by the power of his mind.

THE CLOCKS THAT COULD NOT BE WRONG

In the nineteenth century, there were two great sources of accurate time in Paris, and they always agreed, even if they were wrong! The two sources were the Paris Observatory and the Eiffel Tower; the Tower sent out time signals so that people could set their clocks and watches correctly. The story goes that one day the Directors of the Tower and the Observatory met – and discovered that the Tower set its clock by telephoning the Observatory, and the Observatory set *its* clock by listening to the signals from the Tower!

THE IMPOSSIBLE WATCHES

Pendulums don't work if you wobble them, but in the 1700s watches were sold in which a pendulum could be seen happily swinging from side to side. But the pendulum was a fake: the watch, like all watches at the time, used a spring to keep time: each time the spring coiled and uncoiled it allowed the hands of the watch to move on slightly. But, attached to this spring was what looked like the end (or 'bob') of a pendulum, and as the spring coiled and uncoiled the bob moved from side to side. In those days people were so impressed by pendulums that they thought they were almost magical, and would make any clock – or watch – work better.

DEVIL IN THE BOX

In a house in seventeenth-century England, a Devil came to stay. The servants who worked in the house were terrified by a strange tapping sound that came from a box on a bedroom windowsill. They decided a 'Devill' was inside the box, and tried to throw it into a moat outside, to drown it. But, as if by magic, it was saved from the water by the branch of a tree – which made the servants sure it *was* a devil. But at least it meant Mr Allen, who kept his watch in the box, got it back.

THE INTERSTELLAR WATCH - 1790

If you like astronomy, you could use a watch built in about 1790 to find out where your favourite stars are. The watch, now in the Science Museum, shows when each constellation (group of stars) rises over the horizon, and also keeps track of the Moon's motion across the sky. It warns when eclipses (*see* **The black sun**, *page 107*) are due, and indicates what the tide is doing at various places. And it tells the time too.

ELECTRIC CRYSTALS

Quartz crystals wobble when they are supplied with electricity, and each one prefers to wobble at a favourite speed. These wobbles are very steady, varying by less than a second a year, which means that they can be used to control the hands (or digital displays) of clocks and watches. The first quartz clock was built in 1929, but the first quartz watches didn't go on sale until the late 1960s.

ATOMIC TIME

The most accurate clocks are atoms! The atoms give off radio waves that wobble exactly 9,192,631,770 times a second. So a machine counts the number of wobbles, and when it has counted 9,192,631,770, it has measured a second. This clock is so accurate that, if it could be kept running for a million years, it would have lost or gained less than one second! It is several million times more accurate than a normal digital watch, which loses or gains around a minute a year.

plastic Rubbish!
HEY! WATCH it!

THE TRAPS OF TIME

Scientists are working on a clock that will not lose or gain one second in ten thousand million years. It is called an ion trap, because it uses a magnetic force-field to trap electrically charged atoms called ions, and these trapped ions are used to control the number of times a radio wave wobbles each second. These clocks could soon be so accurate that, if one could have been running throughout the entire history of the universe, it would still be accurate to within one second today.

Quiz

1 To tell the time, ancient Greeks used
a) Their feet
b) Shadows
c) The Sun

2 What type of clock did Columbus use on his ship?
a) A chronometer
b) A sand-glass
c) A sextant

3 Big Ben was silenced during the First World War because
a) It was too inaccurate
b) It was said to attract zeppelins
c) It made beer sour

4 On the Moon, a grandfather clock would
a) Go fast
b) Go slow
c) Float away

5 Clocks have been designed in the shape of
a) Ships
b) Mice
c) Mushrooms

6 The plans for Galileo's clock were found
a) In a butcher's
b) In a baker's
c) In a candlestick-maker's

7 Which of these have been used in clocks?
a) Incense
b) Liquid metal
c) Acid

8 Which is the most accurate
a) A stop-watch?
b) A quartz clock?
c) An atomic clock?

9 If quartz crystals are supplied with electricity they
a) Explode
b) Melt
c) Wobble

10 Japanese clocks used to have movable hour markers because
a) The speed of the clocks changed through the day
b) The length of the hours changed through the day
c) The lengths of the hands changed through the day

CHAPTER 3
Life Time

There were clocks long before there were human beings: body clocks (or biological clocks). These are parts of plants, animals and people which control some of the things they do: they tell flowers when to open, birds when to migrate and people when to sleep.

Your body has all sorts of natural rhythms: 'circadian' rhythms control things that happen each day, like sleeping. But some of your rhythms are faster than this: you breathe every few seconds, your heart beats around seventy times a minute, and your brain waves have pulses lasting less than a second.

Animals and plants have to grow old and die to make way for new generations. Some insects live their whole lives in a few days, while the biggest trees live for thousands of years.

Human beings are probably the only living things with a sense of time: we can remember the past and think about the future in a way that no animal can. We can also use our time-sense to measure how long things take, and even use it as an alarm clock. As we grow up, we learn to use our memories better, and they can be trained to remember an enormous amount: but nothing like as much as we forget!

EYES IN THE TOP OF YOUR HEAD

How many eyes have you got? Answer: three! You, and other animals too, have a third eye in the middle of your brain, called the pineal gland, which is connected to your other eyes and is part of your body's system of clocks. These clocks control the changes that take place in the body at different times of day – so that you are tired at night and ready to wake up in the morning. Millions of years ago the pineal gland might have been an extra eye – or pair of eyes – which could see normally. In birds, fish and some reptiles it reacts to light directly.

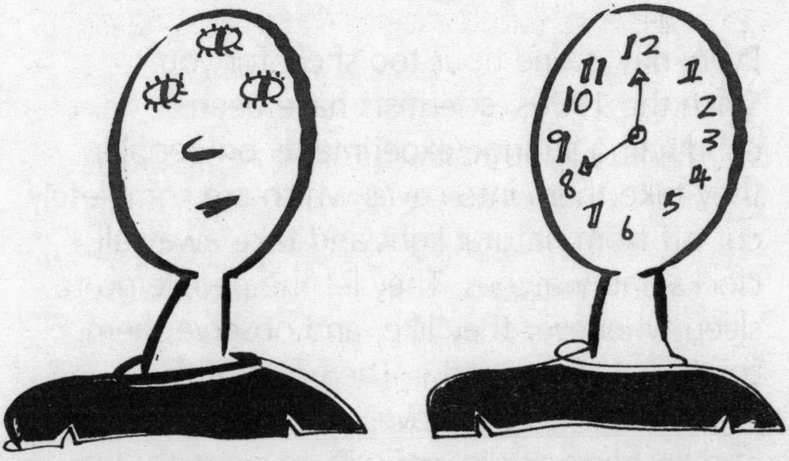

THE ALARM IN YOUR HEAD

Your body's system of clocks can do lots of things: it can instruct the body when to be tired or hungry, estimate how much time has passed, and tell what time it is. You can even use it as an alarm clock: if you concentrate on the time you want to wake up, just before you go to sleep, you should wake when you want to. In experiments, people were kept away from clocks and watches for forty-eight hours and then asked what they thought the time was – some of them were right to within half an hour.

BODY TIME

Every day is one hour too short for you. Since the 1930s, scientists have been conducting strange experiments on people: they take them into caves which are completely cut off from natural light and take away all clocks and watches. They let the people go to sleep whenever they like, and observe them, sometimes for months. The point of the experiments is to discover more about the way human body clocks work. To begin with, the people get tired every twenty-four hours as usual, but gradually they begin to go to bed later and later, until they settle down to a cycle in which they live a 'day' which is about twenty-five hours long. Experiments like this have been carried out on animals too, and it is normally found that they also have 'natural' days which are longer than real ones.

TIME TO REMEMBER

Your memory for things that have just happened is best in the morning, but things that happened longer ago can be remembered better in the evening. Humans have all sorts of other natural daily rhythms: for instance, you tend to feel sleepy around the middle of the day, and your body temperature is lowest at about 4 a.m. and highest at about 4 p.m.. There is also a natural rhythm of alertness throughout the day, in which people are most wide-awake about every one and a half hours or so. Even while you sleep, this rhythm continues, with periods of light sleep followed by periods of deeper sleep.

DOES YOUR BODY CLOCK MAKE YOU SAD?

Do you hate dark winter days? Some people are really depressed by them, and the reason is that their body clocks are wrong! What *should* happen is that, every day, sunlight sets the clocks so that the body knows what it should be doing. But bright light is needed for this, and in winter there may not be enough, so the clock is not set properly and people feel tired and depressed during the day. This 'Seasonal Affective Disorder' (SAD for short), can be cured by treatment with special bright lights.

BOILING YOUR HEAD

In the 1930s, an American scientist called Hudson Hoagland was busily heating people's heads up with special electric helmets. But this wasn't just for fun: he had noticed that when his wife was ill with fever she counted more quickly, and thought that the temperature of the brain might change the way it estimated the flow of time. His experiments showed that people with hot brains really did have a time sense which was speeded up, so that time seemed to flow 20 per cent faster for them.

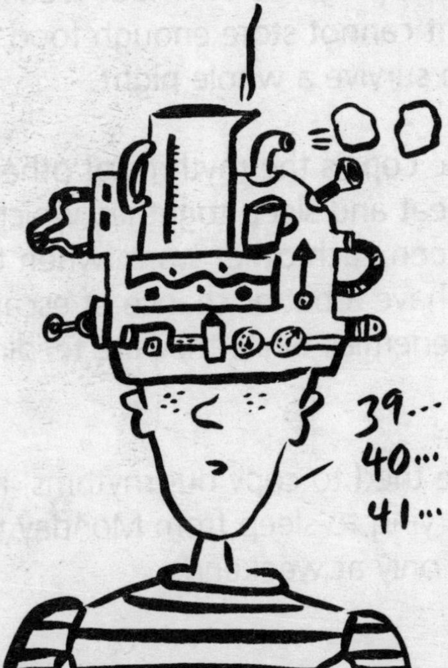

SHORT DAYS FOR SMALL MICE

If you were a field mouse, you'd have to cope with a day that was only three hours long. Many animals, including people, have natural rhythms that fit in with a normal day: people sleep for about eight hours a day and are awake for the other sixteen.

But some animals have different rhythms, and the field mouse lives a three-hour day, spending two hours sleeping and one hour feeding. This is because it cannot store enough food in its stomach to survive a whole night.

Each mouse copies the rhythms of other mice, so they all eat and sleep together, which means that they keep each other warm when they sleep, and have a better chance of escaping from their enemies while they are feeding in the open.

If field mice tried to copy our rhythms, it would be like us trying to sleep from Monday to Friday, and eating only at weekends.

BEE ON TIME

Could you remember to turn up to nine appointments on time each day? Bees can – and they don't even have watches. Instead they have extremely good body clocks, so they can be trained to go to a particular place up to nine times per day. They also use their awareness of the time to work out where they are from the position of the Sun in the sky. They need their accurate time-sense when they visit flowers which only open at particular times of day – due to *their* internal clocks.

AN AMAZING MIGRATION

It would take you a long time to travel 3000 kilometres without a plane, a car or even a bike – but butterflies do it every year. American Monarch butterflies fly this distance from Canada to Mexico and the southern United States each summer, where they hibernate.

In spring the butterflies set off back towards Canada, but stop and lay their eggs on the way before dying. The eggs hatch, and when the caterpillars turn into butterflies, they continue their northward journey towards Canada. All this behaviour is controlled by the butterflies' body clocks.

TIME TO GET UP

In Sri Lanka, flying foxes (a type of bat) have to get up in the morning, because fruit bats will be waiting to use their beds. The bats and foxes have body clocks which keep time with each other, so that they can share the same nests: the bats use them during the day, and leave them to the foxes at night. This means that more bats and foxes can live in an area of forest than would otherwise be possible.

FIDDLING CRABS

Fiddler crabs do what their clocks tell them – even if it makes no sense. These crabs make elaborate displays to attract a mate, running along the beaches where they live, changing colour and waving their claws around. These displays take place at particular times of day, when they are mostly likely to be seen by other crabs. But when fiddler crabs are taken to other parts of the world, their body clocks still keep time with the place they came from, so they will make their displays even in the middle of the night when no other crabs can see them.

THE MOON EGGS

The Moon might not matter much to you, but it is the best friend of a small fish called the grunion. The grunion lays its eggs on Californian beaches, but only for a few hours after high tide, and only on a few nights following a full or new Moon. Because the tide is high, the eggs can be laid a long way up the beach and they will be left to develop *above* the water line, safe from being eaten by other fish. But when the eggs hatch, the young fish need to be able to swim away: and the Moon looks after this, by making an extra high tide at just the right time to meet the hatching eggs.

CLOCK WITHOUT HANDS

In 1745 a Swedish scientist called Carolus Linnaeus invented a working clock with flowers instead of hands. The internal clocks in some plants make them open and close their flowers at particular times of day, and by planting different varieties of these plants together, Linnaeus had a clock – to tell the time, all he had to do was see which flowers were open. The clock worked from 6 a.m., when the spotted cat's ear opened, until 6 p.m., when the evening primrose opened. It also included African marigolds (which open at 2 p.m.), and scarlet pimpernels (which close at 2 p.m.). In 1998, a new version of the flower clock was patented in Holland.

WE TOLD YOU TIME AND TIME AGAIN – HANDS OFF the CLOCK!

IF YOU WANT TO KNOW THE TIME, ASK A POTATO

Potatoes can tell the time, and predict the weather too. The rate at which potato plants use oxygen changes through the day. Even when they are cut off from all outside changes of light, temperature, air-pressure and humidity, they still take in most oxygen at 7 a.m., noon, and 6 p.m.. It has even been found that the amount of oxygen they use depends on the air pressure – and not only the air pressure at the time, but the air pressure the day before *and* the day after!

JUST ANOTHER CENTURY TO WAIT ...

All sorts of plants flower every year, but the Chinese bamboo flowers only once every 120 years! How does it know when 120 years have passed? Scientists think that the plant can measure the length of the day. Each spring, when the days get longer, the plant 'knows' a year has passed, and when it has counted 120 springs, it flowers. Chinese bamboo plants that live near the equator often flower many years late, because the days there are a similar length all year, so it is difficult to tell when it is spring. It is hard to study these plants, because they live so much longer than people.

THE WATCH IN YOUR WRIST

Before good clocks were invented, people sometimes used their pulses to time things. The Italian scientist Galileo Galilei probably used this method to time the first pendulums in the seventeenth century. You can feel your own pulse if you rest your fingertips lightly on the inside of your wrist or on your throat. The trouble with using the pulse as a timer is that it changes depending on what you do – it goes faster if you have been exercising, and also when you are ill.

THE SPEED OF TIME

Do your older relatives say that the weeks go by too fast? They're right! And if you think it's a long wait from Monday to Friday, you're right too. As people get older, time seems to go by more quickly. Older people's bodies work more slowly than those of children – their hearts beat slower, their reactions are not as quick and wounds take longer to heal. So it may be that their body clocks slow down too, so the world seems to move faster.

DREAMTIME

You will probably spend at least five years of your life dreaming, at a rate of about two hours a night. When people dream their brain activity changes, so it is possible to measure the actual time dreams take by using a machine to monitor the brain. Although some dreams seem to last a long time, actually a lot may be added to a dream when it is remembered, to fill up gaps in the 'story' the dream tells. Some dreams last only a second or two, although very long dreams can take more than half an hour.

WHEN YOUR MEMORY WAS YOUNG

Your memory is three years younger than you are. Most people's memories start to work properly when they are about three – you probably can't remember much that happened before then. As you grow up, your memory improves and you forget less: over a few months, six-year-olds forget nearly twice as much as adults, and nine-year-olds forget about one-third more than adults. Memory starts to get noticeably worse again after about sixty.

I REMEMBER ...

The longest number ever memorised had 42,195 digits. This was the number of digits of the number pi that were memorised by Hiroyuki Goto in Tokyo in 1991 (pi is the number you would get if you measured the distance around a circle, and divided it by the distance from one side of the circle to the other). If the numbers he memorised were printed in this book, they would fill the next 30 pages. But even he couldn't have memorised all the digits of the number pi: it goes on forever!

REALLY BAD MEMORIES

Can you remember yesterday? Some people can't. There is an illness called Korsakov's syndrome in which people can only remember things that happened a long time ago – they may not be able to remember their last meal, but think that things that took place years ago have only just happened. In fact, their memories of distant events are far better than those of people with normal memories: it is as though a whole period of time has been wiped from their minds.

EDIBLE MEMORIES

I'VE JUST EATEN A BRILLIANT IDEA....
HOPE IT WAS BETTER THAN LUNCH!

Have you ever thought of eating your teachers instead of listening to them? If not, you might just want to try it: it has been discovered that flatworms can obtain the memories of other flatworms by eating them! To make this weird discovery, scientists first trained flatworms to avoid a bright light, and measured how long it took them to learn. They then minced up the worms and fed them to other worms (who luckily aren't too fussy about what they eat). When the scientists shone bright lights on them, the worms avoided them much more quickly than an average worm did. It is thought that this tendency to avoid the light was 'recorded'

in big molecules which don't break down in the worms' stomachs. Human stomachs do break down molecules like this, so we can't really learn by eating clever people. Which is probably just as well.

SLEEPTIME

Why do your parents make you go to bed earlier than they do? It's because you really do need more sleep. When you were born, you needed sixteen hours of sleep per day, but as you got older, you needed less: fourteen hours at four months old, twelve hours at two-and-a-half, and now you need between nine and eleven hours, and your parents need about eight. When you are in your sixties, you will only need about seven hours.

ANIMALYMICS

The fastest mammal, the cheetah, can run at 100 kilometres per hour. Some birds can move much faster than this: the fastest is the peregrine falcon, which can reach 200 kilometres per hour when it is swooping. But the slowest mammal, the three-toed sloth, normally moves at under 2 metres a minute. At a sprint, it can manage 4.6 metres a minute – more than 300 times slower than the cheetah.

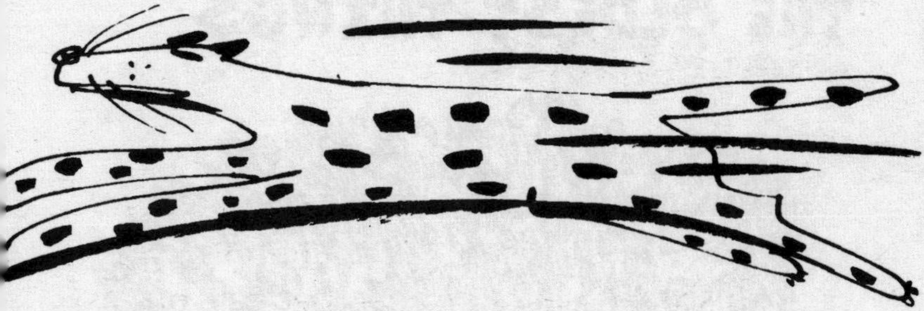

A LIFE IN A DAY

Only the very oldest mayflies have lived a whole week as adults. Most of them live only a few days, or even a few hours in some cases – though they spend two or three years as a larva at the bottom of a lake or stream first. But one type of wasp lives its whole life, from egg to death, in a single week. Not all insects have such short lives though: ants, bees and termites live in groups, with lots of workers looking after a single queen, who spends most of her life laying eggs. These queen insects live for a long time: queen bees live for more than six years, queen ants more than fifteen years and queen termites may live more than fifty years – more than two and a half thousand times as long as the short-lived wasp.

THE OLDEST THINGS

HAPPY
12,000 th
BIRTHDAY

The oldest living thing is more than a thousand times older than you are.. It is a redwood tree, which lives in California and is at least 12,000 years old. It is nearly six metres wide, over 72 metres high, and is called 'Eternal God'.

People live longer than most animals – one in ten thousand people live to be over 100, and a few people have celebrated their 120th birthday. But a few animals live even longer than this – giant tortoises can live for over 150 years, and clams may reach over 220.

THE HEART-BEAT COUNT-DOWN

Why do mice only live about two years? Perhaps because they've run out of heart-beats. There is a theory that most mammals have about two billion heart-beats in their lives. Big mammals like elephants and whales have hearts which beat slowly, so it takes them many years to reach two billion beats. Small mammals like mice and shrews have hearts that beat more quickly, so that they only live a few years. But humans, and other mammals with big brains for the size of their bodies, have hearts which beat more than this: a human heart beats about three billion times in a lifetime. There are many theories that explain why this might be.

Quiz

1 If you heat your head up
a) Your time-sense speeds up
b) Your body-clock stops
c) You lose your balance

2 Every year, the American Monarch butterfly flies
a) Thousands of kilometres
b) Hundreds of kilometres
c) Dozens of kilometres

3 The grunion lays its eggs near high tide
a) To make sure they don't dry up
b) To make sure other fish don't eat them
c) So that it knows where to find them

4 During your life, how long will you spend dreaming?
a) About five weeks or so
b) About five months or so
c) About five years or so

5 The number pi is
a) Three digits long
b) 42,195 digits long
c) Infinitely long

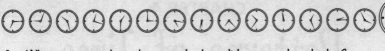

6 When you were born, how much sleep did you need each day?
a) About eight hours
b) About sixteen hours
c) About twenty hours

7 A queen ant lives
a) About a week
b) Less than two years
c) More than fifteen years

8 Which lives longest:
a) A giant tortoise
b) A redwood tree
c) A clam

9 The Chinese bamboo normally flowers
a) Once a year
b) Once a decade
c) Once every 120 years

10 SAD stands for:
a) Seasonal Affective Disorder
b) Stressed And Drowsy
c) Sunlight Acquired Disease

CHAPTER 4

Patterns of Time

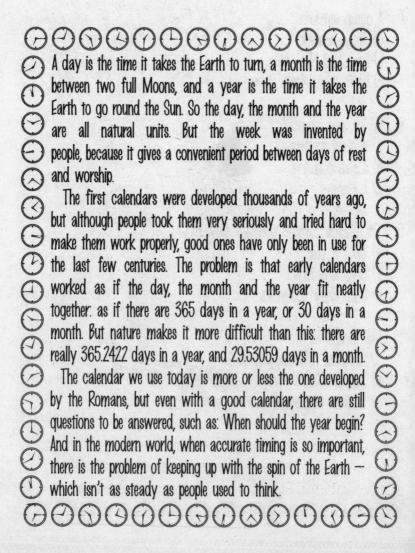

A day is the time it takes the Earth to turn, a month is the time between two full Moons, and a year is the time it takes the Earth to go round the Sun. So the day, the month and the year are all natural units. But the week was invented by people, because it gives a convenient period between days of rest and worship.

The first calendars were developed thousands of years ago, but although people took them very seriously and tried hard to make them work properly, good ones have only been in use for the last few centuries. The problem is that early calendars worked as if the day, the month and the year fit neatly together: as if there are 365 days in a year, or 30 days in a month. But nature makes it more difficult than this: there are really 365.2422 days in a year, and 29.53059 days in a month.

The calendar we use today is more or less the one developed by the Romans, but even with a good calendar, there are still questions to be answered, such as: When should the year begin? And in the modern world, when accurate timing is so important, there is the problem of keeping up with the spin of the Earth – which isn't as steady as people used to think.

HOW MANY CALENDARS?

THE DATE? HUMMM... ACCORDING TO THE NILE THIS MORNING...
AND the STARS...
AND THE FACT THAT it's BEEN FOUR FULL MOONS SINCE THE DEATH OF RAMESES...
EGYPT

If you took a trip in a time machine and asked some ancient Egyptians what the date was, they might give you three answers. Farmers depended completely on the Nile, the river that runs through Egypt: they ploughed and sowed when the water level fell, harvested when the river was at its lowest, and celebrated when it flooded. So they used a calendar based on the level of the Nile waters. The priests had a calendar based on observations of the stars, which they used to work out the timing of festivals and magic ceremonies. And politicians used a third calendar, based on the time that had passed since the last King came to power.

CHRISTMAS IN AUGUST?

Would you like to have Christmas a bit earlier each year? All you have to do is adopt the Muslim calendar. This calendar is based on the Moon, which changes from full to new to full again in about 29.5 days – a lunar month.

There are about twelve lunar months in a year. But there aren't *exactly* twelve, so dates in the Muslim calendar start about eleven days earlier each year – and if you used this calendar for the next eleven years, you could celebrate Christmas in August.

AD IS BC

Christ was born about four years Before Christ! BC stands for 'Before Christ', and AD stands for 'Anno Domini' – which means 'in the year of our Lord', i.e. after the birth of Jesus Christ. So it should be very easy to work out when Jesus was born: AD 1. Unfortunately, an error was made hundreds of years ago in calculating the date of Jesus' birth, which means that it probably happened in about 4 BC! The BC/AD dating system was not developed until hundreds of years after this, by which time an error of a few years didn't make much difference.

APRIL FOOLS?

The original April Fools were probably people who celebrated the new year on 1 April. In France until 1564, the year started then, and people used to celebrate and have parties and exchange presents. Then the King adopted a new calendar, starting each year on 1 January. Not everyone was happy with this, and some people kept celebrating on 1 April – but their friends made fun of them, and thought they were April fools.

NAMING THE YEAR

The Sioux Native Americans gave years names instead of numbers. Not like 'Graham' or 'Nicola', but 'The year of the solar eclipse,' 'The year of the meteor storm,' or 'The year a trader brought guns'. The Sioux drew a picture each year to show what had happened. Although giving names to years like this means that you can't do sums with them, it does make sure that historical events are recorded.

WHAT'S THE TIME, MR WORM?

Most people use the TV or radio to tell them the moment at which each new year has started. But the Trobriand Islanders of New Guinea use worms.

These worms appear on the surface of the sea between 15 October and 15 November – they react to the light of the full Moon during that period.

When the islanders see them, their year begins with great celebrations, and everyone has lots of fun, except for the worms. They get eaten.

WHEN AM I?

Italy in the thirteenth century had three years at a time. Different places used to give different numbers to the year: so when it was 1245 in Venice, it was 1244 in Florence and 1246 in Pisa.

Luckily, most people only dated things by the day of the month, not the year – and when they did refer to a year it was normally by the number of years that had passed since the last king came to power.

WHAT LEAPS IN A LEAP YEAR?

A leap year has 366 days instead of 365. Leap years are needed because it takes the Earth slightly more than 365 days to go round the Sun. So if every year had only 365 days, the date would get out of step with the Earth's movement round the Sun. To avoid this, we make every fourth year 366 days long, by adding an extra day on to the end of February. Each normal year begins one day of the week later than the last: so if a normal year begins on a Monday, the next year will end on a Tuesday. But if a leap year begins on a Monday, the next year will 'leap over' Tuesday to begin on a Wednesday.

THE LONGEST YEAR

One year, New Year's Eve was delayed by ninety days. Once Julius Caesar (or rather Sosigenes, the astronomer who worked for him) had invented his nice new super-accurate calendar (*see* **The Roman conquest of time**, *page 84*), he had to deal with the fact that the old one had allowed the dates to slip until the 'official' midsummer day took place ninety days before the real one. He added all these days to the year 46 BC, making it 455 days long. No wonder people called it the year of confusion!

DIFFERENT SEASONS

In many countries, there are four seasons: summer, winter, spring and autumn (or fall). The date on which each starts is when something special happens to the day: summer starts with the longest day, winter starts with the shortest day and spring and autumn start when day and night are each the same length. But other people have different seasons: the Eskimos have five, the Salteaux Native Americans have six, and a Sudanese tribe called the Nuer only have two.

THE LONG NIGHT

In the Arctic and Antarctic, there is no Sun in midwinter, and no night at midsummer. All over the world, except at the equator, the days are longer in summer and shorter in winter. In European and North American winters, the Sun rises later, stays lower in the sky, and sets earlier than in summer. The further north you go, the lower the Sun is in the sky in winter and the shorter the days are. During the winter in the northern parts of Russia, Scandinavia and Canada, there are days when the Sun never rises, and at the North Pole itself, the Sun is not seen at all for nearly six months. The reason for all this is that the Earth spins at an angle to the Sun, and the North Pole is tipped so far in winter that the Sun is hidden.

THE ROMAN CONQUEST OF TIME

In 46 BC Julius Caesar gave the world an excellent calendar – and Augustus Caesar took it away again. Before Augustus, the Romans had sorted out all sorts of problems with the calendar and ended up with months which formed a tidy pattern of days: 31, 29 (or 30), 31, 30, 31, 30, 31, 30, 31, 30, 31, 30. But one month was named Julius after Julius Caesar, and Augustus demanded that the next month was renamed after him and made the same length. This messed up the other months, and gave the weird order we use today: 31, 28 (or 29), 31, 30, 31, 30, 31, 31, 30, 31, 30, 31.

HAS THE MONTH STARTED YET?

It is easy for us to say when a month starts, but the ancient Hebrews found this quite a tricky question to answer: for them, the month did not begin after a certain number of days had passed but only when the new Moon was first spotted. Once the priests had sighted the Moon, they would light a fire on a hilltop, and as soon as it was seen other fires on other hills would be lit, and in this way the message that the month had started would travel hundreds of kilometres in a few minutes. The beginning of the month was an important event, because the dates of holy days were based on it. But not only did cloudy nights cause problems, sometimes fake signal fires were lit too. Finally, when the Romans banned the use of these signal-fires altogether, the Hebrews developed a new system which did not depend on seeing the new Moon. Instead, a new month was begun every 29 or 30 days.

ONCE IN A BLUE MOON

There really are 'Blue Moons', except that they're not blue! The saying 'once in a Blue Moon' is used to describe a very rare event, like England winning the world cup. Actually Blue Moons happen a lot more often than this: when there are two full Moons in a single month, the second one is called a Blue Moon. This happens about once every three years. A far rarer thing to happen is a month without a full Moon: the last time this happened was February 1999, and the next one will be February 2018. By which time, England might even have won the world cup again!

HOW LONG IS A WEEK?

SCHOOL
THE WEEK WAS INVENTED SO THAT THEY CAN GET RID OF US FROM MONDAY TO FRIDAY...

How long does a week last? Seven days? Or ten? Throughout history, weeks with all sorts of different lengths have been used. One week, used in West Africa long ago, was four days long, and there were ten-day weeks in Ancient

Egypt and in France following the French Revolution. The week is an odd length of time because, unlike the day, the month or the year, it is not based on any natural event. However, people have found it useful to have a time which is longer than a day and shorter than a month, and most have chosen seven days. Seven days might have been chosen because the Moon changes from new to half full in about this time, or because the number of known planets, plus the Sun and the Moon, used to be seven.

A REVOLUTION IN TIME

TOLD YOU THIS MONTH WAS SLIPPY!

Imagine having to wait eight days for the weekend. During the French Revolution, the revolutionaries wanted to change the way time was measured. They decided to have a hundred seconds in a minute, a hundred minutes in an hour, ten hours in a day, ten days in a week (which was called a decade), three weeks in a month and twelve months in a year. For a while people used some of these ideas in France, but they didn't like them. The months were given official names like *Germinal (seed time)*, *Messidor (harvest)* and *Floréal (blossom)*, but British people soon started to call them *wheezy*, *slippy* and *drippy*. After a few years, everyone was so tired of the system that Emperor Napoleon Bonaparte put a stop to it.

TRAVELLING TO YESTERDAY

You can have two birthdays next year: all you need to do is go to Siberia for your birthday. The next day, fly east to Alaska, and it will be your birthday again. This is because you have crossed an imaginary line, called the International Date Line, which runs up the Earth between America and Asia. It is one day earlier east of the line than west of it. In Jules Verne's book *Around the World in Eighty Days*, the travellers kept careful count of the days and discovered that they had taken eighty-one days to go round the world. This meant they had lost their bet – or so they thought until they discovered that they had 'saved' a day because they had travelled in an easterly direction.

THE SLOWING PLANET

The days are longer now than they were thousands of years ago, because the Earth's spin is gradually slowing down. The reason is that the gravity of the Moon raises tides on the Earth's oceans which act like giant brakes to slow the Earth down. This means that on average each day is about one-hundred millionth of a second longer than the last one. This is also why we always see the same side of the Moon: the pull of the Earth has stopped the Moon from turning away from us. It still rotates, but it now takes the same time to do so as it does to go around the Earth. As well as this permanent gradual slowing, there are quicker changes in the Earth's spin too, which can make the days either longer or shorter for a while (*see* **The time police**, *below*).

THE TIME POLICE

There is an organisation of time police in France which keeps an eye on the motion of the Earth, and keeps clocks in time with it. It's not easy to tell, but the Earth does not turn smoothly – and when the Earth wobbles, the day's length changes. There are lots of reasons for this, including the gravity of the Sun and Moon, the amount of ice at the North and South Poles, and changes inside the Earth. Even the weather has an effect: in January 1990 high winds blowing from India increased the length of the day by 1/2000 second. When the Earth's day has stretched enough, the time police order that an extra second, called a leap second, is added to the length of the year. Since 1972 there have been more than 20 leap seconds, which are added either in June or December. One of these extra seconds was added at the end of 1998, delaying the start of 1999 by one second.

TIME BY NUMBERS

We have sixty seconds in a minute and sixty minutes in an hour because 60 is a magical number – or so the Babylonians believed, 4000 years ago. It was the Egyptians who decided to divide the day into twenty-four parts: though the hours they used were not all the same length, as ours are today (*see* **The long hours**, *page 35*). It may be that 60 and 24 were thought to be special because they are so easy to divide up into smaller numbers.

SMALL TIME

The word *minute* does just mean a 'minute' (i.e. very small) fraction of an hour. The *second* used to be called the 'second minute', which just means 'a smaller fraction' of an hour. Although seconds and minutes were invented thousands of years ago, they were only of any use when clocks became good enough to measure them: so minute hands only became common from about 1660, when clocks had pendulums. Some clocks were given second hands at about the same time.

Quiz

1 The minute gets its name because
a) It is a 'minute' piece of time
b) It is the time taken to dance a minuet
c) It was invented by Mr Minute

2 During winter at the North Pole, the Sun is below the horizon for
a) One week
b) Exactly half the time
c) All the time

3 Which occurs more often, a month with two full Moons, or a month with no full Moon?
a) A month with two full Moons
b) A month with no full Moon
c) They both occur equally often

4 The Trobriand Islanders start their year when
a) Worms appear on the sea
b) Grunion eggs hatch
c) American Monarch butterflies appear

5 The longest year was
a) 46 BC
b) 4 BC
c) AD 1564

6 If it is Saturday in Alaska, what day is it in Siberia?
a) Friday
b) Saturday
c) Sunday

7 Thousands of years ago, the days were
a) Longer than they are now
b) Shorter than they are now
c) The same length as they are now

8 How many calendars did Egypt have?
a) 1
b) 2
c) 3

9 46 BC was called the year of confusion because
a) It was very long
b) It was very short
c) It was really AD 46

10 The original April Fools were probably
a) People who celebrated two birthdays a year by flying across the international date line
b) People who thought the Earth was slowing down
c) People who celebrated New Year in April

CHAPTER 5

Exploring Space and Time

Until this century, people thought that time was just part of the background of life. Things happened *in* time, but time itself just flowed on like a river. Albert Einstein realised this didn't make sense, and he discovered that time itself can change and be affected by all sorts of things. He also found that there are different times for different people. Since Einstein's discoveries, scientists have found out more about the nature of time, and some of them now think that time travel may be possible.

Throughout history, as people have found out more about the Sun and the planets, they have discovered that there are natural time-cycles throughout the solar system. The Sun has a rhythm of changes that take about eleven years, and each planet has a day and a year of a particular length.

This century, it has been discovered that the whole universe has developed over time from its birth billions of years ago, and scientists are now able to look forward and study the way the universe will end.

THE BEGINNING OF TIME

Time probably began about fifteen billion years ago. Scientists think that if there were no stars, planets, people or anything else, there would be no time, so time probably started when the universe began. How do they know when this was?

Astronomers have found that the parts of the universe are all moving apart, as if they all started in the same place. Because they know how far apart the parts of the universe are now, and how fast they are going, they can work out roughly how long ago they must have been together – and the answer is about fifteen billion years.

Although almost all scientists now agree that the beginning of the universe was a gigantic explosion called the 'Big Bang', the details are still uncertain.

CAPTAIN'S LOG, STARDATE ...

On *Star Trek*, Captain Kirk calls his diary a log for the same reason boats measure speed in knots. Each ship used to have a real log and the sailors used it to chart their ship's progress in a very simple way: by throwing it overboard!

There was a rope attached with knots tied in it. As the ship moved away from the floating log, the sailors measured how much rope was pulled away in a certain time (measured by a sand glass) by counting the knots. The number of knots the sailor counted in the time gave the speed of the ship.

5-4-3-2-1 ACTION

Why was the countdown invented? To make things more exciting! Every space-craft launch today, whether of a satellite, a space probe or a space shuttle, begins with a countdown. The first countdown took place at a rocket launch in 1929 – but it wasn't a real launch, it was in an early German science-fiction film called *The Woman in the Moon*. But everyone thought it was such a good idea, they've used it ever since!

EARTH CALLING SPACE

Messages from Earth have reached thousands of stars already. Humans started sending radio messages to each other in the 1890s, and TV pictures in the 1920s. Radio and TV signals don't just travel between places on Earth, they go through space too – much faster than any spacecraft. So alien creatures might be watching our TV programmes even now! If there are any aliens living near the closest star (which isn't very likely), any radio or TV signals from Earth they can pick up will be about four years out of date, because of the time it takes the signals to travel that far. The signals would also be extremely weak and any alien would need amazing technology to pick them up and watch *Star Trek*.

ARGHHH !!!
I'VE LOST STAR TREK!

THROUGH THE LIGHT BARRIER?

Light travels over 900 thousand times faster than sound so you hear thunder after you see lightning. This means that you can easily tell how far away a thunderstorm is, by counting the seconds between the lighting and the thunder. If you divide the answer by three, that gives the distance in kilometres, because sound travels at about 0.33 kilometres per second – which is about one kilometre in three seconds. When a plane goes faster than sound, people say it has broken the 'sound barrier'. Because nothing can go faster than light, the 'light barrier' is unbreakable (*see* **Backwards in time**, *page 21, to find out why*).

ANCIENT WEATHER

Trees contain records of the weather thousands of years ago. They grow at different speeds through the year, which means the wood inside them changes colour, so if you cut a tree down (it might be a good idea to ask first though!) and looked at the trunk you would see a series of rings, one for each year. Counting the rings gives the age of the tree, and more can be found out be measuring how thick each ring is. Wet weather makes the tree grow faster, so the rings it makes are thicker. Pieces of some ancient trees have narrow rings caused by the effects of a volcano on the weather between 1160 BC and 1140 BC.

HOW OLD IS THAT GLOW?

If archaeologists want to know how old a piece of pottery is, they put some of it in an oven and watch it glow. The brightness of the glow gives the age of the pottery.

There are several other ways archaeologists use to date things – they especially like measuring the amounts of different substances in ancient objects, because these substances change into others over long periods of time, so the amount left tells them how old the object is.

WAIT FOR IT

Glass is a liquid, and you could pour yourself a cup of it – if you waited. One thing that makes glass different from other liquids is time – if we could speed time up, we would see glass flow.

You get the opposite effect if you do a belly flop in the swimming pool – the water has no time to move out of the way, so it feels like hitting the ground, because water, which we know is a liquid, is behaving like a solid.

TRAVELLING TO TOMORROW

Want to visit the future? Try sleeping on it – close your eyes and suddenly it's nine hours later. Hedgehogs, tortoises and bears sleep through the winter, and fleas can sleep for months until food (like you for instance) comes along. If a person could do something like this, and go to sleep for months or years, it would be as if they had travelled into the future when they woke up. When insects and small animals get cold enough, they can 'sleep' indefinitely, and some people have had themselves frozen in the hope that they can be revived one day – when they have travelled into the future.

THIS ATOM WILL SELF-DESTRUCT IN TEN SECONDS

There are lots of materials which decay with time. Their atoms are so big that they can't hold themselves together, so they disintegrate, leaving behind smaller atoms, and energy (the energy is formed from some of the matter that made up the original atom). The 'half-life' of a material is the time it takes for half of the atoms in a lump of material to disappear in this way. One type of lead has a half-life of about half an hour, but one type of uranium has a half-life of over four billion years.

THE SHIFTING EARTH

Part of the Science Museum in London ignores the Earth's spin. A pendulum 22.45 metres long hangs down the stairwell near the café, and swings slowly from side to side all day – but it also does something strange. As the day goes on, the direction in which the pendulum swings gradually alters. Or so it seems. Actually, it is not the pendulum that changes direction – it is the Earth, which turns slowly *under* the pendulum.

It is called Foucault's pendulum, after the scientist who invented it.

CATCHING THE RAYS

Is the Sun nearer to the Earth in the summer or winter? Both! It is winter in southern countries while it is summer in northern ones. The distance of the Sun varies by five million kilometres through the year, and it is nearest to the Earth at the beginning of January, but this isn't what causes winter and summer. The reason winters are cold is that the Earth is tilted away from the Sun then, so the Sun is lower in the sky. This means its rays are spread out more than in summer, so the heat and light are less concentrated.

THE ASTRODATE

If you decide to take a trip in time (*see* **Time machines** *page 112, or* **Travelling to tomorrow**, *page 104 for some ideas*) how will you know the date when you stop? You could always work it out from the stars: the Earth's North Pole points at a star called Polaris at the moment, but over the centuries it changes and points at different parts of the sky, taking 26,000 years to get back to Polaris again.

If archaeologists are lucky enough to find accurate pictures of the night sky in ancient ruins, they can use them to fix a date. Once they were really lucky – they found a carving showing the Moon and planets as well as the stars, and worked out the day on which the carving had been made – it was 7 July, 61 BC.

THE BLACK SUN

When the Moon covers the Sun, night can fall in the middle of the day. The Sun is 400 times further away from us than the Moon, and 400 times bigger – so they are the same size in the sky, and the Moon can exactly cover the Sun and cause a total solar eclipse. The Earth is the only place in the solar system from which these total solar eclipses can be seen.

Some stone circles like Stonehenge can be used to predict eclipses, and ancient civilisations like the Maya knew when to expect them too. They thought they were dangerous, so they had to know when to hide!

SOLAR CYCLES

What do trees, the weather, and spots have in common? The answer is the Sun! The Sun goes through a regular series of changes each eleven years – its face gets covered with spots and storms on its surface get more intense. This activity has effects on Earth: the temperature rises and there is more rain, so trees grow more quickly. It has even been suggested that the stock-market is affected by this cycle, and that riots and revolutions are more likely when there are more sunspots too.

PLANETARY TIME

A day is 9.8 hours long, and there are more than 10,000 of them in a year – on the planet Jupiter. A day is the time it takes a planet to turn around once, and a year is the time it takes to travel once round the Sun. The closer a planet is to the Sun, the shorter its year is, because it has a shorter distance to go round the Sun than a more distant planet, and because it needs to go fast to avoid being dragged down by the Sun's gravity. So on Mercury, the nearest planet to the Sun, a year is only 88 Earth days long, but on the furthest planet, Pluto, a year takes more than 90,000 Earth days (so birthdays there must be really exciting!) Jupiter's day is the shortest of any planet in the solar system, while a day on Venus lasts 243 Earth days.

WARP FACTORS

There really are warps in space and time. In fact, you're making one now! For a long time gravity was a mystery – how could one thing (like the Earth) pull another (like the Moon) without actually touching it? Then Albert Einstein suggested that what happens is that all objects bend, or 'warp' the space and time around them, and this disturbs the way other objects move. The more massive the object, the more space and time are warped. Einstein predicted that these warps would affect light rays, and he was proved right in 1919 when scientists measured that the Sun bent starlight that passed close to it by just the amount that he predicted.

THE PARTICLES THAT COULDN'T BE

Every day, particles which only last two microseconds last sixty microseconds – it depends on who is counting! These particles are called muons, and they are created high in the sky and then shoot towards the Earth. Scientists can work out that each muon can only live for two microseconds, and yet it takes about sixty microseconds for them to reach the Earth. So does a muon last for two microseconds, or sixty? Both! Because these particles travel so fast, time passes more slowly for them, and if they wore little watches they would only measure two microseconds while those of people on Earth measured sixty (*see* **Time for everyone**, *page 19*).

STOPPING TIME

Gravity slows down time. Accurate clocks on the ground run measurably slower than similar clocks on planes because the gravity on the ground is stronger than high in the air where the planes fly. If gravity is strong enough, time can even stop completely. There is a type of star which has so much gravity that nothing can escape from it, not even light. Because no light can get away, these stars are black, and are called black holes. If you watched a spacecraft approach a black hole, you would see the astronauts on board move more and more slowly, until, when the spacecraft reached the edge of the black hole, the astronauts would not move at all because time would have stopped.

TIME MACHINES

THAT'S NOT WHAT I MEANT WHEN I SAID WE NEEDED A WORM HOLE!

Scientists can't build a time machine – but they know what one might look like. It would be like a pair of dark openings hanging in space, each surrounded by a glow of light. Rockets would take people through one opening and emerge from the other in the past or the future. The openings would be connected by an invisible something called a wormhole, which is a corridor through time and space (and which sometimes appears on *Star Trek!*). Time machines like this could be made by warping time and space (*see* **Warp factors**, *page 110*) – the trouble is, scientists would need the technology to move planets around to manage it!

ACCELERATING TIME

The universe is about six thousand times older than the human race. If everything was speeded up so that the whole history of the universe from its creation to the present day took place in one week, the first atoms, and light, would appear during the first minute. The first stars would form on Monday, but the Sun would not develop until Friday afternoon. The Earth would form on Friday evening, and life would begin early on Saturday morning. Human beings would not evolve until late on Sunday night, two minutes before the end of the week, and they would only learn to make fire during the last minute of the week. And you were born in the last one-thousandth of a second before the end of the week.

THE FATE OF THE UNIVERSE

In the end, the universe will probably just fade away. At the moment, it is growing as its galaxies move away from one another, but as time goes by this growth is slowing down. It is possible that one day the universe will stop getting bigger and start to shrink again, until there is a 'big crunch', after which a new universe might start. But the theory which best explains the latest observations of the stars is that the universe will just go on growing. As it does, the stars will reach the ends of their lives, and explode or fade away. Gradually the universe will get darker and colder until there is no more light. Long after this, trillions of trillions of years in the future, the atoms that make up the universe may fall apart and only tiny particles will remain.

RUNNING OUT OF TIME?

When will time end? Never. There is no reason to think that time will ever come to an end – even if everything else does. Time, space, matter and energy all seem to be linked, so that they must all exist together. Although stars and atoms may all fall apart one day, there will always be something left in the universe, however cold, black and empty it becomes. So time itself will probably go on forever too.

I'VE GOT ALL THE TIME IN THE WORLD FOR YOU....

Quiz

1 Ships measure speed
a) In knots
b) In logs
c) In nautical miles

2 Total eclipses of the Sun are visible from
a) All the planets
b) Only the Earth
c) Venus, Mars and the Earth

3 The Sun is nearest to the Earth
a) In January
b) In June
c) In October

4 When do scientists think time began?
a) Never
b) About 15 billion years ago
c) About 4.6 billion years ago

5 You would find a Foucault's pendulum in
a) A grandfather clock
b) The Science Museum
c) Foucault's house

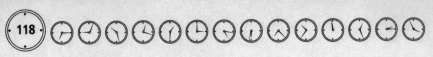

6 The countdown was invented in
a) The 1920s
b) The 1940s
c) The 1960s

7 What does a plane break to make a sonic boom?
a) The sound barrier
b) The light barrier
c) The time barrier

8 Which are liquids at room temperature?
a) Glass
b) Mercury
c) Wood

9 A half-life is
a) The time it takes for half the atoms of a material to decay
b) The time it takes for a planet to go half-way round the Sun
c) The time it takes a person to reach middle age

10 When will time end (probably!)?
a) In about a billion years
b) In about fifteen billion years
c) Never

Quiz Answers

CHAPTER 1

1 - b, 2 - a, 3 - a 4 - b and c, 5 - b,
6 - a, b and c, 7 - a, 8 - b, 9 - b, 10 - b

CHAPTER 2

1 - a, b and c, 2 - b, 3 - b, 4 - b,
5 - a, b and c, 6 - a, 7 - a, b and c, 8 - c
9 - c, 10 - b

CHAPTER 3

1 - a, 2 - a, 3 - b, 4 - c, 5 - c,
6 - b, 7 - c, 8 - b, 9 - c, 10 - a

CHAPTER 4

1 - a, 2 - c, 3 - a, 4 - a, 5 - a,
6 - c, 7 - b, 8 - c, 9 - a, 10 - c

CHAPTER 5

1 - a, 2 - b, 3 - a, 4 - b, 5 - b,
6 - a, 7 - a, 8 - a and b, 9 - a, 10 - c

Index

If you have enjoyed this book, look out for:

THE SCIENCE MUSEUM BOOK OF AMAZING FACTS

WEATHER

Anthony Wilson

It's a breeze! Read on for a feast of weird and wonderful facts about the weather!
You can measure the temperature by counting how fast a cricket chirps.
Your hair is slightly longer on a damp day than on a dry one.
There's a town in Chile where it didn't rain for 14 years.
A hailstone the size of a melon fell on Kansas, USA in 1970.
Bad weather may have helped wipe out the dinosaurs 66 million years ago.

If you have enjoyed this book, look out for:

THE SCIENCE MUSEUM BOOK OF AMAZING FACTS

COMMUNICATION

Sarah Angliss

Get wired with a feast of weird and wonderful facts about communications!

All the TV and radio ever broadcast is moving continually through space.

Live pictures of Nelson Mandela's release from prison in 1990 will soon be reaching Sirius, a star over 83 billion kilometres away.

The Internet is the descendant of a military secret message-carrying system, designed to survive a nuclear war.

Over 34 million computers are sold every year – but when IBM first made them, they thought they'd be lucky to sell more than five.

If you have enjoyed this book, look out for:

THE SCIENCE MUSEUM
BOOK OF AMAZING FACTS

DISCOVERIES

Beverley Birch

For trailblazers – a feast of weird and wonderful facts about discovery – old and new.
Rotting sugarbeet gave the first clues to the causes of killer diseases.
A small girl playing in caves found Ice Age paintings over 17,000 years old.
Radioactivity first revealed itself on a cloudy day in Paris – in a desk drawer.
Peering into rainwater puddles, a curious linen-draper discovered the invisible world of living creatures that surrounds us.

If you have enjoyed this book, look out for:

THE SCIENCE MUSEUM BOOK OF AMAZING FACTS

INVENTIONS

Beverley Birch

For bright sparks – a feast of weird and wonderful facts about inventions.
The inventors of the first robot were put on trial for witchcraft.
In the 1700s, dead men's teeth, taken from skulls in graveyards and battlefields, were used as false teeth.
The first electric light bulbs needed a health warning: 'Do not try and light with a match.'
The first working television was made from a knitting needle, the lid of a hatbox, an electric fan motor, and torch batteries, all put together on top of an old tea-chest.

If you have enjoyed this book, look out for:

THE SCIENCE MUSEUM BOOK OF AMAZING FACTS

ENERGY

Anthony Wilson

Power up – a feast of weird and wonderful facts about energy!

If your legs were as powerful as a flea's, you'd be able to jump over an 80-storey skyscraper.

In 1986 two Japanese motorists drove right across Australia without using a single drop of fuel.

There's enough energy in one flash of lightning to power all the lights in a typical house for a year.

You can warm up a cup of coffee just by stirring it.

SPORT

by Colin Jarman

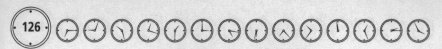

No sweat – a feast of weird and wonderful facts about sport!
A modern tennis racket is so light that the heaviest part is the glue holding it together.
Long jumpers can leap further at the equator than they can at the Poles.
A squash ball hit at 240 kilometres per hour will rebound off a wall at only 65 kilometres per hour ...

CONSTRUCTIONS

Chris Oxlade

For towering intellects – a feast of weird and wonderful facts about constructions!
Mosquitoes brought the building of the Panama Canal to a standstill.
The suspension cables of New York's Brooklyn Bridge contain enough steel wire to stretch across the Atlantic four times.
Tunnelling machines owe their design to the teredo worm, which burrows through damp wood.
The Great Pyramid held the record for the world's tallest building for nearly four thousand years.

If you have enjoyed this book, look out for:

THE SCIENCE MUSEUM BOOK OF AMAZING FACTS

EXPLORATION

Anthony Wilson

For far-out kids – a feast of weird and wonderful facts about exploration!
People in ancient Peru thought that the Earth was square.
Christopher Columbus kept a false log book so that his men wouldn't find out how far from home they really were.
In 1960, a balloon bigger than St Paul's Cathedral was launched to study cosmic rays.
You can't have a boiled egg for breakfast at the top of Mount Everest because boiling water doesn't get hot enough.